#SUNNYMOTIV

THE SUNNY SERIES

VOL 1

Written by Sunil K. Osman
First Edit by Martin Abdalla Kalunga
Second Edit by Pritima Kassan Osman
Layout and Design by Roshan Kassan
Final Edit by Lauren Mooi

First published by LAUREN MOOI Publishing 2020

Copyright © 2020 by Sunil Osman

All rights reserved. No part of this publication may be reproduced, stored or transmitted in any form or by any means, electronic, mechanical, photocopying, recording, scanning, or otherwise without written permission from the publisher. It is illegal to copy this book, post it to a website, or distribute it by any other means without permission.

Sunil Osman asserts the moral right to be identified as the author of this work in accordance with the Copyright Act 98 of 1978
First Edition. Volume 1. July 2020 in paperback

ISBN: 978-0-620-88909-4

www.laurenmooipublishing.com

#SUNNYMOTIV

THOUGHTS & MUSINGS
FOR YOUR SOUL

Acknowledgements

To my parents, grandparents and every other person that has influenced my life to this present day, this is for you. This is also for the people who inspire me and those I inspire too. I further honour and appreciate my Angels and Guides who work tirelessly to ensure that I am in divine alignment in pursuit of my Soul's purpose.

Preface

The very first #SUNNYMOTIV was made public on my Twitter platform at 09h22 on the 23rd of October 2011. The tweet went as follows, "Forget the silver lining, beyond the clouds are bright rays of sunshine…" I recall the reason behind those words being triggered by regularly hearing people speak about a "silver lining". This made me stop and realize, that many people seek the silver lining within those proverbial clouds, whereas in actual fact the sun beyond the clouds shines brighter and stronger than anything that anyone can ever imagine. And that is the sole purpose of this book, to help people see beyond their silver lining and onto something much more meaningful. It is also meant to inspire those who have lost inspiration and to encourage those who have lost their courage. Each quote was perfectly designed to speak to not only your mind, but your heart and soul as well. #SUNNYMOTIV encourages you to re-evaluate your life, where you are now and where you would like to be. It aims to bring light and comfort to you when you need it most, and firm advice when you don't want to hear the truth. Enjoy the journey as you go along, and don't forget to take some time to reflect on all the lessons learnt.

How is a #SUNNYMOTIV created?

It is pivotal to understand that I do not simply create any of the #SUNNYMOTIV. Nor have I taken another person's quote and claimed it as a #SUNNYMOTIV. I am open to learning any approaches taken by others. I am inspired by other people who through their motivational words and actions and their good deeds share their light with the world. On the one hand, I am able to tap into a state of being that is remote, very deep, intense and spiritually defined as my personal space. And on the other hand, I am able to tap into a wild, silly and very playful state. I explore my facets equally and bring that flexibility to my work and world.

My #SUNNYMOTIVs come from within, often my motivational chambers unlock when I am reflecting on life through meditation or through an upsurge of motivational energy ignited by the inspiration around me. This inspiration comes from people, nature, sound, taste and visual aesthetics. Whenever I tap into my element, which happens frequently, I explode with #SUNNYMOTIVs.

The Sun Will Rise – 2008

I wrote a rather euphoric note on Facebook, on the 9th of November 2008 at 07h26. In fact, I consider this piece as an extended #SUNNYMOTIV. I felt that my soul had awakened to full awareness and that I was in full control of my physical actions. I love being in the constant state of being pro-active, and I realized in my transformed state to my present high self-state, I could have and should have started posting #SUNNYMOTIVs a long time ago.

To everyone who have given themselves the opportunity to read my book, make a promise to yourself that you will not wait a life time to liberate your spirit, for you are perfectly and wonderfully made, you are authentic, whole and indivisible from birth and that this is the truth for all. Be yourself.

SO... THE SUN WILL RISE

It was in the morning at 05h03 to be exact. A friend woke me up who needed to talk. Before the conversation I decided to do something, I had not done in a long time. I got dressed, pulled out my car and took a drive to the beach to witness the sun rise. As I arrived, I parked my car alongside the beach and sat in a calm state of mind watching the waves crashing over and over on the smooth shore. For quite some time there was no sign of the sun, the skyline was just cloudy with traces of a light orange glare reflecting on the ocean. That was my hope; this glare of light cemented a strong belief that the Sun will eventually rise. I then drifted my focus towards the beautiful scenery, observing birds flying without restriction, while I listened to the harmonious combination of the sound of wind and water splashes. I took it all in and everything gave me the impression of a beautiful orchestra. In a sudden occurrence, I saw a glimmer of light looming from behind the cloudy skyline. Immediately within me ignited a surge of excitement and I smiled. It was the sun, and it was rising like I had believed it would. Now as this beautiful natural process was taking its course, everything got frantic. The birds got louder, waves crashed harder and the fishermen around developed a sense of urgency. I was infested by the same vibrational frequency, thus I also rushed to pull out my camera and the frequency of my energy suddenly became tranquil. I tried to make sense of what may have caused the sudden energy shift I had experienced (from a high frequency of energy to a sudden peaceful state). But then I realized that, nothing around me had changed, besides the appearance of the rising sun. I took a deep breath, balanced my energy and re-aligned my focus to my surrounding and further enjoyed the beautiful scenery; the birds, the ocean, the waves, the mountain and most importantly the sun rays glittering on the waters of the sea, which made the waves far lovelier than they were before. When I was a child, I was often told that, with great care and patience things get better with time. Bear in mind that, I had been there for quite some time since my arrival and I live to testify the truth about that saying because, everything just looked brighter after some time. Nature was taking its course. Nature was in union with its natural dwellers. Therefore, I always keep this to heart. No matter how deep is the depth of your sorrow, how mute is your silence, how desolate is your sadness and how dejected is your depression. THE SUN WILL RISE AGAIN. No matter who you have fought against, who may have ripped your heart into shreds, which you cannot stand, and whom you long for… THE SUN WILL RISE AGAIN. Symbolically, after your life's misfortunes the sun will rise again meaning that, in life every painful encounter comes to healing and no matter the duration of your suffering, it will eventually come to an end and when the time comes when the sun rises again in your life make sure you absorb, balance out and unify the beauty and the bold aspects of your life lessons. You are a beautiful Soul.

How to read "The #SUNNYMOTIV"

This is not your normal conventional book; you may start at any section as you please. Take life as an example, every person makes their own choice. I employed the same approach with this book. I enjoy it when people use the option to exercise their free will; I mean is that not the essence of living? The idea behind a #SUNNYMOTIV is to provide words that will comfort and heal the human soul and heart, to express and give teachings of gratitude and address and provoke emotions of spiritual nurturing and mentorship in all spheres of human existence. Therefore each #SUNNYMOTIV will carry its own authentic translation, or you can search for a #SUNNYMOTIV that is pleasing to your spirit and heart. I want to offer healing to the world, and this is my way of producing the vaccine using my spiritual antidote to the universe. All I ask of you while reading this book, is to take a lesson from a #SUNNYMOTIV that resonates with you and use it accordingly in your daily life. Furthermore each #SUNNYMOTIV will occupy its own page. This is because each will give sufficient daily meditation space to allow your being to radiate with light and divine positive vibrations.

Your dreams can take you anywhere and everywhere if you let them.

Why do we dream? Is it because a dream allows you to be anything you want? Or is it because dreams come true? Have you ever considered that dreams are only but a vision of what your reality is capable of becoming? Well, it's true. Your dreams may invite the idea that allows you to be anything you want, but it is you who will make it possible. You see, dreams are like a short movie trailer. There's only enough to entice you, which leaves you wanting to know more. But sadly, that's all your dream can offer. If you want to know how the movie ends, you have to buy the ticket. The first step to living out your dreams is realizing that you actually want that more than anything else in the world. The second step is knowing how to begin. Once you know how to start living your dream, the rest becomes a challenge and not an obstacle. Challenges are things that make you great, it is opportunities that will test your endurance, your mind and capabilities. Giving up on those opportunities before trying creates an obstacle. When you say yes, you have accepted the challenge. But when you say no, you have created an obstacle. The one thing I love about dreaming, is the fact that you already have the idea on how to achieve it, because you wouldn't be dreaming it if you didn't know what to do next. So, start letting your dreams take you everywhere!

A LOT OF LIFE COMES DOWN BELIEF AND INTENT

This is mainly about doing what you deem as a spiritual or religious practice, in a way that is comfortable for you. Notice how society will set conditions and normalize "best practices" of how individuals should do certain things or perform certain practices. If you are not, how comfortable do you feel within your soul about any of these considered "best practices". Then is it really the best practice for you? Let me make an example; If I bath using coarse salt instead of Epsom salt, and I bath with the intention of cleansing my body on a cellular level; will the bath not work? Of course, it will. Another example: If I light sage incense made by hand versus sage incense which was factory produced, and I light this sage incense with the intention of cleansing my space, does that mean it will not work? The moral of these examples is to encourage you to do whatever you believe is positive for your spirit and watch your world transform around you. We are often told how to pray, meditate, do yoga or practice and live out different faiths. If you find that your personal practice and your intentions is of the highest and supreme positivity then keep doing this, because every action has an intention, make sure it is positive and pure of heart.

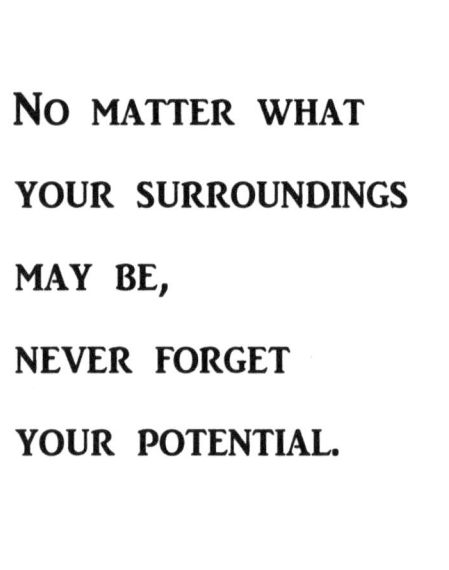

No matter what your surroundings may be,
never forget your potential.

I ask that you vividly visualize a rose bud and then one that has just bloomed. Now add very green yet tattered leaves that have been eaten by worms to both roses. Some people allow their surroundings or circumstances they have been brought up in, define who they are and where they will end up in life. But I say to you, do not allow that to be you. Visualize the two roses again. They both have leaves around them that have been eaten away. These roses were both buds at the same time, but the one bloomed despite its surroundings and eaten leaves. Now are you going to be the rosebud that remains closed or are you going to be the rosebud that opens up all its glory despite its surroundings? It is mainly about being patient with yourself in achieving your full potential. Never let your surroundings overwhelm you. Be the rose that blooms no matter what. How many times have you just felt terribly down? Or everything you do or choose turns out SO negatively? Instead of allowing that negative outcome to consume you, rather choose to allow it to empower you.

This is one thing that is a lot easier said than done. One of the most difficult things to do is think positively in a negative situation. Positivity is a state of mind. Thus, anyone can choose to tap into that state, at any given time. It is the ability to think differently when in a negative situation. The best way to create your own positivity is get rid of your negativity first. How you ask? Simple. Any way the negative energy pushes you. If you feel like crying, then you should cry. If you feel like screaming, then you should go ahead and scream (preferably in a pillow, it's much more satisfying). And if you feel like breaking something then go on and break something (preferably nothing too expensive). But be sure to do all this in the privacy of your own home or bedroom. The last thing you need is someone telling that you can't express your negative emotions because that's a lie. You need to get rid of those feelings/thoughts/energy that is weighing you down, so that you can make room for all the positive. Once the negative leaves you, you will not only feel so much better but you will quickly realize that everything that has gone wrong has passed and you are now in a position to look forward to the good things that are coming your way. And you will be able to see it, because positivity happens naturally when you make room for it.

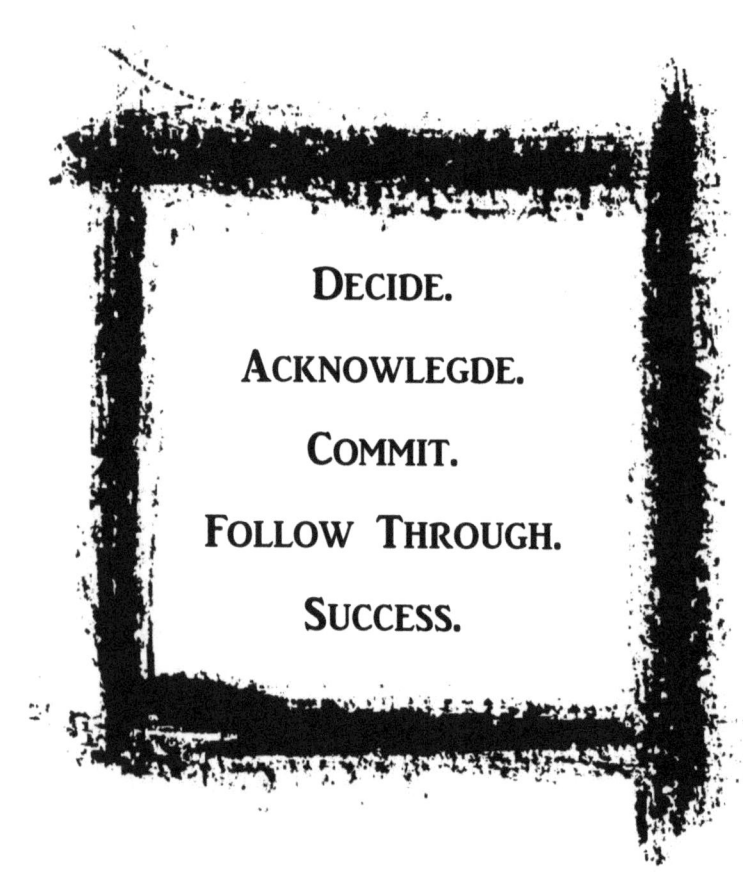

In business, most people decide within the first 5 seconds of meeting you if they are going to do business with you or not. There is a similar concept in life. People generally make a decision on how they see you within the first few seconds of meeting you. So, it is up to you to decide how you want people to see you and how you want people to interact with you. Make that decision first thing in the morning, then acknowledge the decision you have made and the outcome you want to achieve. Commit to that image and follow through. If you keep doing this every day, it will lead you to success. Once you have mastered who you would like to be; confident, charismatic, smart, a leader, the world becomes your oyster and you can achieve just about anything. But it all starts with you and how you want to be seen in this world. So, I encourage you to make decisive decisions that are fit for you, as often as you can. Then allow those decisions to bring you success.

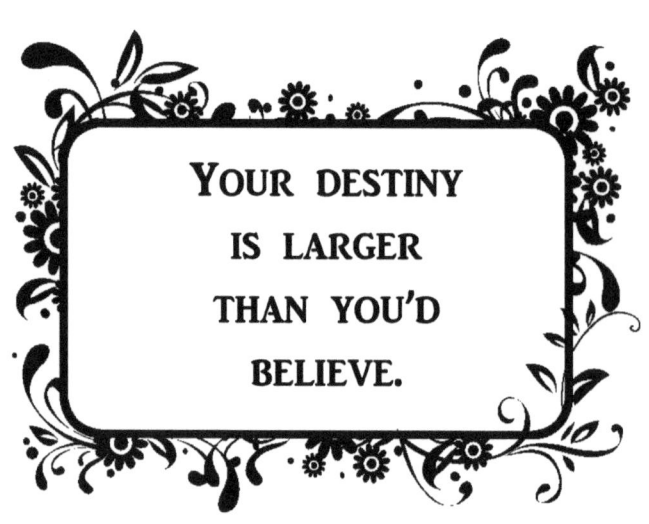

You shouldn't allow what you think your destiny is, to limit you because your divine plan could be bigger than you may ever imagine. If you have a burning desire to be more than what you are now, do not let your circumstances or surroundings stop you from believing that you are worth more. Keep pushing to achieve those goals and never take your eye off that desire to be more. You will become what your destiny says you will be, as long as you don't give up. Once you have achieved your first set of goals, I encourage you to create new goals and also change paths. You will realize that the destiny you may have envisioned originally becomes completely different. This is all part of life's journey. Embrace it. Many believe that no matter the path you choose, your destiny will always fall into place. It's what you do with that information that will determine the best outcome for you. So here is a thought, what is your destiny and what path have you chosen?

When you try and make someone happy and they just never are, it's not your fault. Happiness comes from within, don't forget about yours.

You cannot force happiness into a space where it is not accepted. Happiness is a state of mind. You can choose certain things to bring you happiness. Like ice-cream, or a comedy show or good company after a long day's work. Once you have decided on the things that make you happy, you will never lose it. People make the mistake by thinking someone else can bring you happiness, that is incorrect. Someone else can bring you joy but your happiness depends solely on you. For example, in relationships, too often one partner tries everything deemed possible to bring the other happiness, but it never works. This could be one of two reasons. The partner receiving the "happiness" may not recognise it has something that they decided on what makes them happy, or the one bringing the happiness may be the one who is actually not happy at all. Never expect your partner to make you happy if you never told them how. Also, don't blame the other for not being happy after everything you have done, because it definitely isn't you. It's their situation that is making them unhappy. Rather encourage them to go and do what makes them happy and ask them if you can join. You never know, their happy place might just become yours.

Every morning that you wake up, is an opportunity to be great. The way you dress and present yourself speaks volumes. The sad reality is, people trust what they see first and not what they know. I could meet you in my PJ's for the first time, and you won't know that I am the founder of BMW, for example. And at first glance, you won't respect me as such because I don't look the part. I know dressing well all the time can be draining, so I suggest you decide when the appropriate time is. For example, if you are going for an interview, you would dress up very formal and presentable because any interview is an opportunity to sell yourself as though you were your own business. And the company interviewing you, requires your services. If you are chosen for the job, you should respect your decision to look presentable and treat your employer as your client. In this way, you will continue to uphold the image you decided on to look professional, and your work will reflect the same. Just because you work for someone else, does not mean you cannot represent yourself as the CEO of your business. Because you can. Know your worth.

Get over shizz and move on. Life is too short to dwell.

If someone does something to betray you or hurt you, the best thing for you is to forgive them and walk away. Forgive especially because they won't ask for it. Holding on to that pain will only kill you faster. And that's what makes life short. When you keep remembering all the bad, you end up living for all the bad. Revenge is never okay, not for you, not for anyone and especially not for your spiritual well-being. You won't ever be okay until you let go and move on. I know it is easier said than done, but at least promise yourself that you will try. Nothing is more difficult than forgiving someone who isn't sorry, but it is possible. If you want to live your life to the fullest, sometimes you just need to let things be. To let go of the things you cannot change is the bravest thing you could do. Walking away from things that cause you pain is the strongest thing you could do. But actually, just doing it is the only thing you need to do for you. It is important to know when to put yourself first, and once you have realized that, you won't allow anyone else to hurt you again.

Respect your hustle, no matter who says what

No matter what your choice is, don't listen to the running commentary. If you have decided to make a living in a way that is unconventional and legal, or not the "standard" way of doing things, you will receive some critics. And that's okay, everyone needs a few critics, because without criticism how will you know when you have succeeded? Criticism allows you to grow in what you are doing. Yes, we don't like to hear negative comments about the way we chose to make a living, but in most cases, we do listen to what is been said, and in turn this inspires us to do even better. In other words, if you do not agree with what is been said, you are driven to prove everyone wrong. That leads to success. Just because something does not work for one person, that does not mean it won't work for you. If you want it bad enough, go get it.

This is about embracing every day that you are graced with. Take each day as an opportunity to be great and do great. You might wonder what it feels like to be awesome, if you don't feel that way already. Well, it simply has to do with being the best you can be with the gifts you have been blessed with. Waking up is a norm, but the moment you realize that it is not just another day, that will be the moment when you can smile and be awesome. Never underestimate the power of a smile. Whether you work for a boss, work for yourself or perhaps you are trying to find the business you should be part of, always smile and walk as though this is the first day of the rest of your life.

**LOVE WHAT YOU DO
SO YOU CAN LOVE AND
RESPECT YOURSELF**

I have said it before that life is short, and in this case, there is no exception. In order for you to truly live a life you can be proud of; you have to love what you do. How you may ask? Stop doing what society tells you to do. Finish school. Go to university or college. Get a degree, so that you can get a good job. Get married. Have kids. Put them through school. Retire. Grow old and die. It doesn't have to be this way. You don't have to have a degree to start a business, you can just hire someone who has one to run it. You don't need a degree to be an artist or an actor or performer. All you need to do is practise until you're perfect and then don't give up until you land that big role or raised enough money to open your art gallery or publish a best seller or create your first clothing line. Whatever it may be, you don't need to follow society's rules on how to live if you have a burning desire to do things differently. Each and every one of us have a unique talent that will set you apart from the rest. Use your talent to discover what it is that you love doing. And just do that instead. Love what you do, by doing what you love.

BE THE PERSON THAT SAYS, "I'LL STAY IN TOUCH" AND ACTUALLY DOES

How many times have you heard or even said the words, "Stay in touch"? And how many times has this phrase been followed through with? I, for one, make a point to go the extra mile and stay in touch with people. With modern technology it is really not that hard to do this. Think about the time you said you will stay in touch with someone, and then you hear of their passing. Not staying in touch is a missed opportunity to connect with different people. Sometimes this connection is meant to be brief and sometimes it will linger for longer. Therefore, saying you will stay in touch and following through is a task that can be marked as a completed promise. I for one believe in keeping promises. A promise is like energy, if it is not completed then the energy remains stagnant. Stagnant energy is not something anyone should invite into in their space. From a business point of view, saying you will stay in touch and actually doing it is just good business practice. Have you ever sat back and thought about the lives you have impacted, just by staying in touch?

#SUNNYMOTIV

Has anyone ever said, "I am going to quote you on that…" Being the one that gets quoted comes with a lot of responsibility, because it often means you must practice what you preach. Yes, we are only human at the end of the day, and acknowledging this is important too. Be the kind of person that gets looked up to, that influences, motivates and inspires. This seems easy enough for some, but being able to just do it isn't the aim. The aim is to be able to do it with impact. Therefore, take what you say seriously and realize that even if it is something said in passing, some people may live by and hold onto your words. Words and actions are powerful.

LEARN SOMETHING NEW EVERY SINGLE DAY

To learn something new every day is about growing as an individual. Whatever is being learnt should be something significant enough to contribute to your mental and spiritual growth. Decide every day on what you would like to learn. Whether it is a new recipe you saw online, or a game that you can play with your family. Make an effort to learn how to do it, and then just do it. You could also decide on something long term and fun, like taking dance lessons by yourself or with your partner. The possibilities are endless, and the human mind will only grow as far as you will allow it. Don't limit yourself in a limitless world. Learning something new every day is also about learning about you. Discovering who you are and what makes you tick is crucial for spiritual growth. It may even allow you to impart knowledge to others and help them learn something new about themselves. Going a day without learning something new is a missed opportunity that you can never recreate.

This ties in with living life to the fullest and without regret. Again, I say to you, learn to let things go. The things that haunt you, that hurt you, that control you. The things you cannot change but so desperately would like to. Living with regret is like asking to die young, because what's the point. Regret consumes every positive thought you may have and creates a black hole filled with disappointment. That in turn, will destroy any desire to be happy. And you will be left thinking… "What if…", so learn to be better than the "what if I…" question by becoming "I'm so glad I did…" statement.

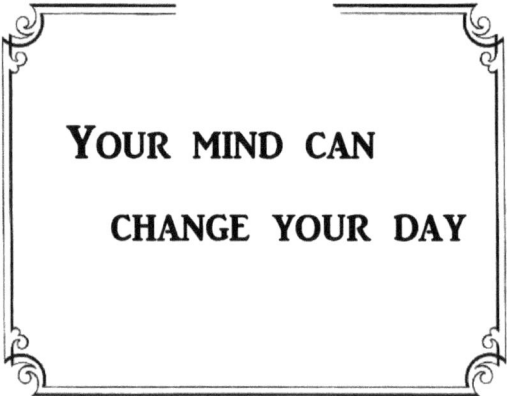

Build your positivity by starting your day with words that can help you set the platform for how your day may turn out. This is not just about saying words like, "I am positive." You have to believe it. Though it may come across as rather odd, but when you truly believe in the words you say to yourself, you will experience a mild shiver from within. You will have raised your vibrations and soon you will start to smile, because your faith in yourself has increased exponentially. That is the rise of chemical levels in the brain and with it the body reacts accordingly.

Start your day with positivity and the words I am...

I stress the importance of positivity, a lot! Because we face a tremendous amount of negative energy every day. And unfortunately, we cannot escape it. That is why we have to practise positive thinking. So, when you wake up in the morning, do not just say the words "I am…" believe in whatever you choose to follow as your words of encouragement for the day. Something simple like, "I am going to have a good day" and believing it can change your mindset. Try it. Believe it. Do It. This is about recognizing your capabilities, by not limiting yourself at the same time.

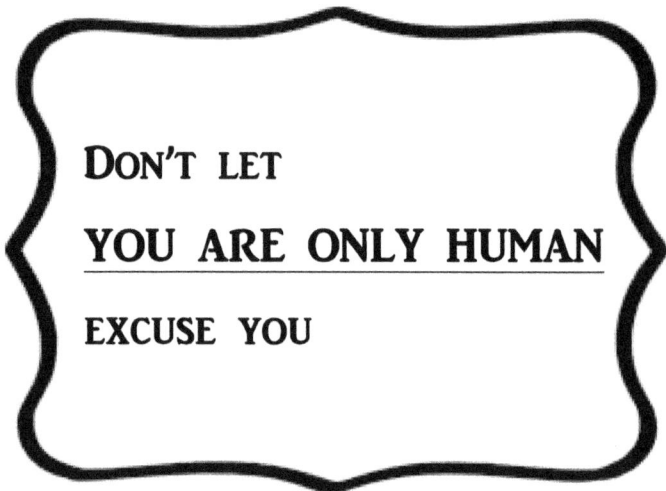

Acknowledging the fact that we are only human, doesn't allow you to use it an excuse to get out of doing something difficult. We all make mistakes because we are human. And while you are trying to achieve your goals, you may step on a few toes and not apologize for it or make things right, and by saying, "I'm only human..." does not make things right. You need to keep pushing yourself to the limits and even past your limits, but you also need to be mindful of your choices and decisions that may have a negative effect on others. It is okay to put yourself first when trying to achieve your goals, but it is not okay to maliciously hurt others while doing so. And by saying you're only human could make you less accountable for your actions. Accepting that you made a mistake and acknowledging it in order to fix the problem is considered as mental, emotional and spiritual growth. And that's where you want to be.

BE STRONG ENOUGH TO BLOCK OUT NEGATIVITY

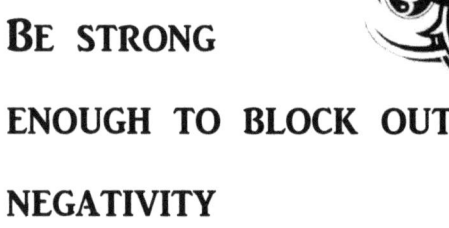

Being in a positive state of mind requires a lot of energy and focus, so it is difficult to stay positive continuously. Especially while living in a world that has negative news reported every single day. Now you may not be able to escape it, but you can learn how to block it out or channel it into positive energy. Every time you hear something negative, ask yourself; does it affect you? How will it affect you? What impact will it have? And do you need to concern yourself with it right now? If you have answered no to all the questions above, then you will have no need to allow the negative to enter into your space. It will be difficult at first, but once you master the distinction, you will find that blocking negativity out will become like second nature, and the easiest thing to do. Always keep focusing on you, your family and your well-being to create continuous positive energy.

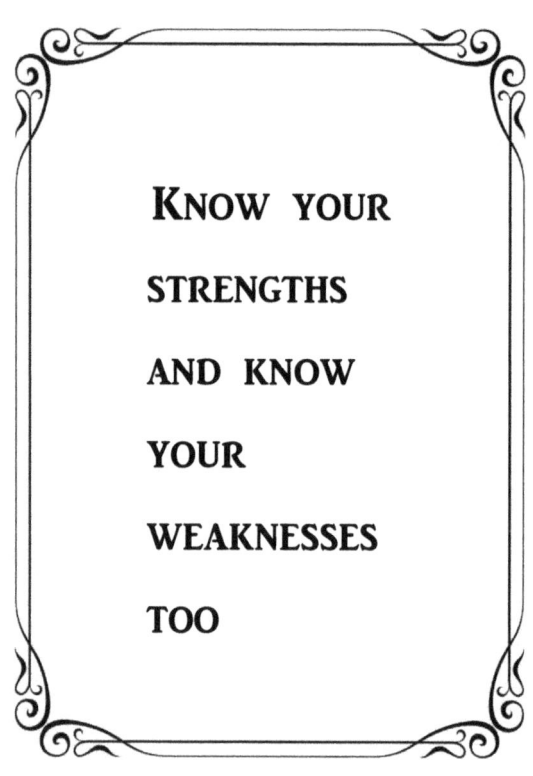

Know your strengths and know your weaknesses too

Strengths come from weaknesses. Let me explain. Before you become good at something, you were really, really bad at it first. And over time with continuous work, dedication and effort, you excelled at what you started. Your weakness has now become your strength. And if you find something that is extra challenging, don't look at it as your weakness, look at it as an opportunity to encourage someone else, who is strong at it. I'll give you an example; I'm not really good at baking but I am excellent at public speaking. Giving up the idea of becoming a baker to become a public speaker is not weak, but rather wise, because it is something I love and enjoy doing. So do not focus on trying to improve on the things that you aren't good it, if it serves no purpose and it is not your passion, but rather focus on things you are good at and become an expert at it instead.

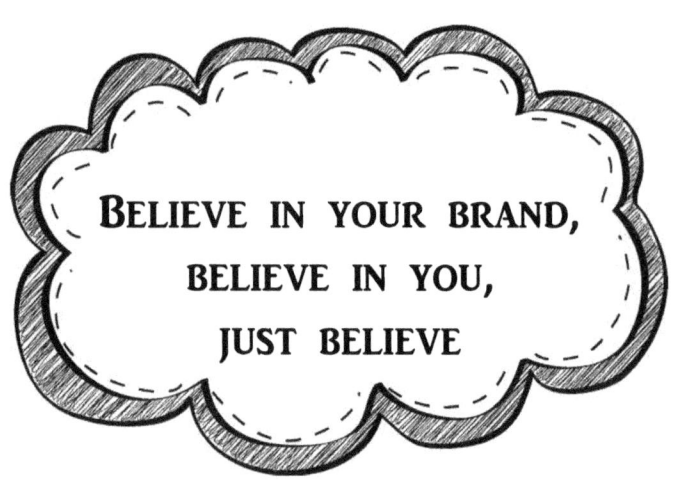

This is more aimed at business than anything else, but it can be viewed from a spiritual perspective too. As an example, I have successively managed to build myself as an Independent Contractor for a very long time and that has allowed me to put together a talk or workshop about running yourself as a Business in the Entertainment Industry. Creating your life and brand seems easy enough in modern times, but is it really? Creating a brand which involves doing all the marketing, building your presentation, making it available all over the internet, and so on is great, but unless you believe in yourself as a brand, your delivery in terms of your marketing and overall presentation counts for a lot. You need to believe that you are good at what you do, AND be good at it. You cannot advertise yourself or your services for something you cannot passionately and potentially achieve nor believe in. Therefore, when you find strength within to believe in yourself and your full potential every task or goal you set to achieve becomes a lot easier.

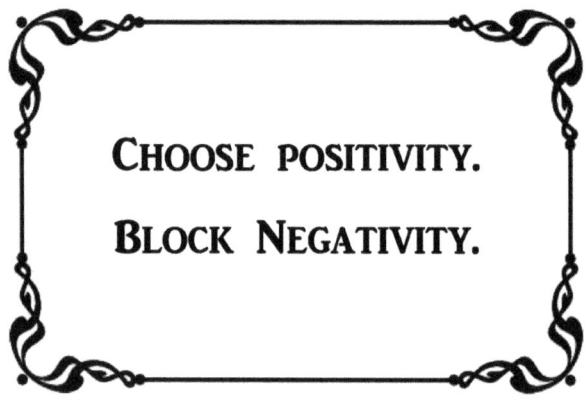

Choose positivity.

Block Negativity.

This is actually harder to do than most people would like to believe. I know we can be as positive as possible and change negative energy into positive energy. You might wonder how easy it can be to actually follow through and keep a constant positive state of mind. When you choose to embody a positive vibrational frequency, you will find that in some situations with negativity all round, you will be criticized, judged and forced to break your vibrational level down to a negative low level. The best thing to do, would be to surround yourself with positive situations, but this isn't always possible. Being aware of the negativity is the best approach here, so you can mentally and spiritually block it out. The results are amazing and you will see and feel the difference if done correctly. The shift will be evident in a way that your vibration increases.

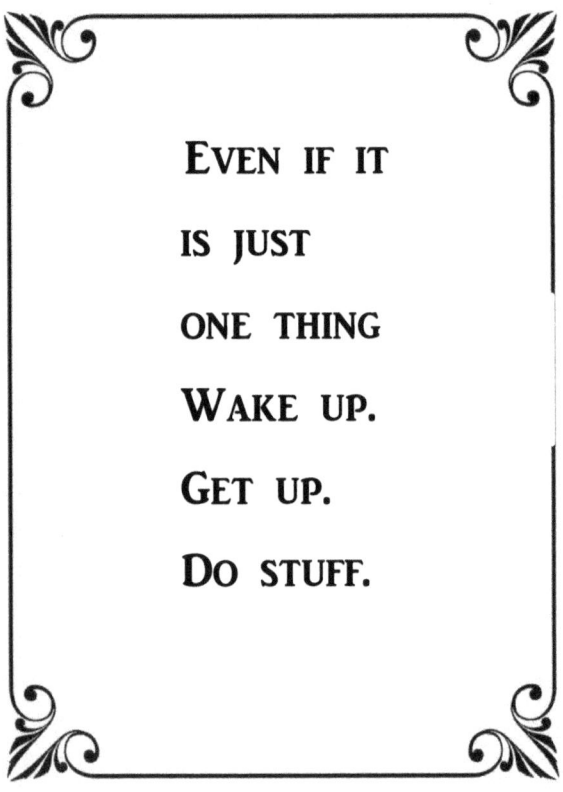

Even if it is just one thing Wake up. Get up. Do stuff.

This is about completing tasks. Every now and then we are consumed by the activities of our daily lives. We focus our energy on many duties. We ought to take each task one at a time, even if it means creating a list of priorities. We have to keep the world going round, because the world needs to be in constant operation. The idea here is to do things and do them well. Too many times when we are consumed by responsibilities, we forget about completing the simplest things with diligence. Never neglect the simple details. Do your duties with sheer brilliance and also do not forget to acknowledge once they are done. Praise yourself on a job well done when appropriate.

Never underestimate the positive energy and power in supporting one another

There is no greater pleasure in seeing people become successful because of something you have advised on or supported them with. We often forget to support each other because we are so consumed with our own success. This is about giving back and also being a Mentor to others. You may be an Accountant, a Lawyer or an Actor, or a member of any other trade or profession but, when you give support and guidance to help someone grow; you cannot help but trigger a surge of positive vibrations within them. I have heard the saying that "your success is my success." And as much as this may be true, it is also about fulfilling your own soul's purpose. Every person on earth will have their own life experience. Some people will grow up with role models, mentors and leaders. So, do not block them off, make sure you give as much as you can without expecting anything in return. This is the greatest thing you can do to raise your vibrations.

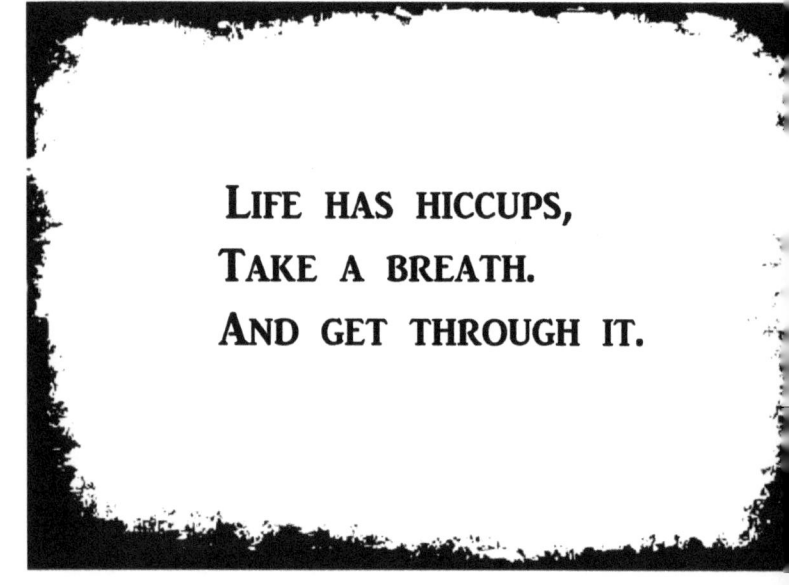

I wish I could say life is really all sunshine and rainbows. But unfortunately, it is not. And we need thunder storms and the rain to understand and appreciate the sunshine and rainbows. Because not everything is set in black and white, there are a lot of grey areas, and that is where trouble lies. When life throws you a setback, take a deep breath, hold on to everything you've got and get through it. Because you will get through it. You were designed to outlast any setback that is thrown your way. You were created to be strong for this very moment, you don't have a choice but to get through it. You can and you will. I know things may look near impossible and I know you can't see a way out, but I encourage you to keep moving. Trust in what you know and keep moving. Build yourself up with positivity and keep moving. Even though it may look like the storm won't pass this time, doesn't mean you have to stay there and wait, get up and keep moving. Because you will come out on top. Difficulties are put in your way to test your resilience and if you believe in your strength, there is nothing that can overcome you.

WAKING UP
SHOULD BE
YOUR
MOTIVATION

This is about appreciating life. Too many times we forget that waking up in the morning is actually a gift. Take important note that waking up each day is more than just a routine. It is a gift that should be embraced, appreciated and cherished. If you embrace this deeply, you already know that you value it as a gift and you will be highly motivated to do great things. Additionally, if you do not value your breath of life, then you need to evaluate the life that you may not like. And ask yourself, why are you not happy? Why would you prefer to be gone instead? If there is a deeper meaning to your answers, I encourage you to talk about it. No matter how real, damaged or sad it may be, you do not have to face it alone. Find someone you trust and confide in them. Every breath you take is important because your life matters.

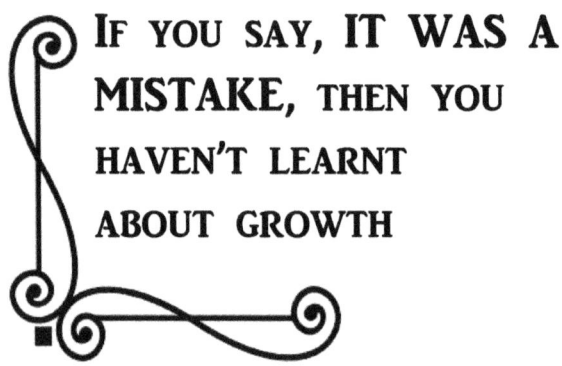

If you say, IT WAS A MISTAKE, THEN YOU HAVEN'T LEARNT ABOUT GROWTH

There's a difference between saying it was a mistake and you learnt from it and saying it was a mistake and you regret it. Learning is our way of growing, and mistakes are part of it. No-one is perfect and I certainly don't want you to think that you have to be either. Because we all make mistakes and rightfully so. Without trial and error, the world that we know today wouldn't exist. So, I encourage you to own your mistakes, acknowledge them, understand them and accept them. Because this shows growth. And always remember that mistakes are there so you can learn from them and never make the same mistake again. Because if you continue to make the same mistakes, then you have not grown. For example, you left a pot of food cooking on high for 45 minutes instead of 30 minutes, and the food at the bottom of the pot burnt. If you keep leaving the heat on for longer than 30 minutes, you will continue to burn the food. However, if you choose to learn from that experience, you will gain understanding and awareness that things need to be monitored and kept in balance at all time. Something as simple as that adds to your mental growth and it will forever remain as a vital lesson learnt. Adopt this into your life and will always grow from your experiences.

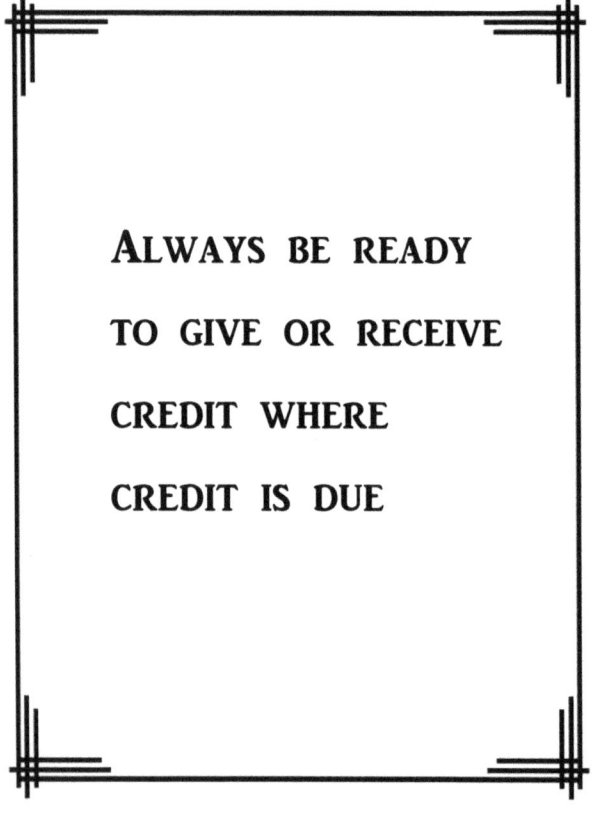

Always be ready to give or receive credit where credit is due

If you have spent hours, days, weeks, months or even years working on something that turned out to be a success, you deserve the recognition. And if it is someone else who has put in all the work, time and effort to achieve success, they deserve their recognition. It is important to understand how life changing recognition can be. Especially if you have invested everything into achieving that goal. Your work deserves credit as much as the next person. When credit is given or received, it creates the feeling of accomplishment. And when you feel accomplished, you looked accomplished. This leads to confidence. And confidence looks like success, even if you are not there yet, looking and feeling the part is always better than the opposite. So, I encourage you to give credit where credit is due as well, so that the next person can experience the same confidence.

Surround yourself with success, and don't forget the ones that want to be surrounded by you. Never underestimate the power of this energy

It has been said that in order to be successful, you should surround yourself with successful people or people with the similar mindsets. Do this even with individuals you aspire to reach and eventually surpass. Always remember, if you are the smartest person in the room, then you are in the wrong room.

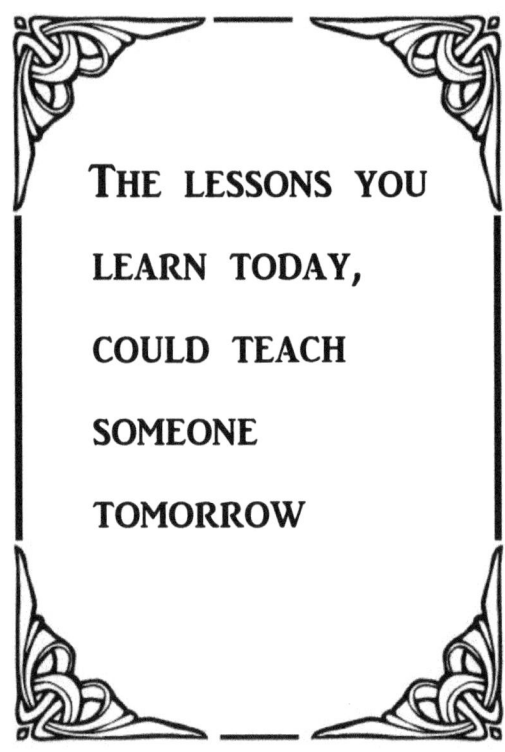

THE LESSONS YOU LEARN TODAY, COULD TEACH SOMEONE TOMORROW

Be fully aware of the individuals that admire you and have an appetite to learn from you and your success or experiences. We are meant to teach one another about what we know so that we may all evolve in this life. This is the very essence of our existence. Therefore, acknowledgments encourage growth. Never forget your purpose, even if it is not clear to you as yet. And always remember what you going through right now, is for the lessons you have to teach tomorrow.

Never underestimate the power of:
1. Meditation
2. Consideration
3. Reflection

When you see the word "meditation", you may assume an environment of complete silence, spiritual candles or quiet pipe music, sitting in deep silence and in deep thought. The truth is that meditation could be merely deep thought about something happening in your life. All true meditation requires is complete focus and intent. If you are in a situation where you need to make a decision, whether it may be life changing or not, the idea is to weigh your pros and cons, and then make the decision you have accepted that is beneficial to your overall well-being. It is vital to reflect on your options before committing to any result. This is not an immediate process, and it is important to take your time when reflecting on options prior to decision making. To a certain degree this process may seem simple for some. However, to be able to simplify the thoughts in your mind into small compartments of clarity is a mentally draining process. It can drain your energy. It is important to be patient and allow it to reveal itself. Your life will be more manageable and you may surprise yourself.

BE YOUR OWN INSPIRATION AND SUPPORT, THEN BE THAT TO OTHERS TOO

Always bear in mind that life is about learning, but what good are the lessons if you keep them to yourself? There are some lessons learnt which may be purely for you and then there are lessons you learn that are meant to be shared with others. Sharing wisdom or our experiences when learning should come naturally and from a good place. And in some cases, your wisdom may not be accepted or taken seriously, but don't let that discourage you or leave you despondent, continue to support and inspire others. Even if they can't see your support as something they may need right now, just be there until they do. Be the support that you want to receive.

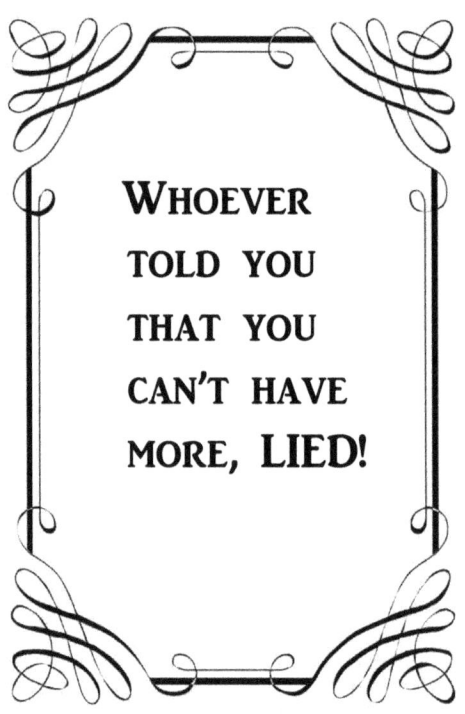

Whoever told you that you can't have more, LIED!

Let no-one convince you that you cannot. Take into account how the human race has evolved over the years. It is our duty to teach and share awareness about these endless possibilities we have come to discover. When you show someone what great results are achieved in taking action, you ignite within them their will power to want to achieve more. Your state of mind can literally change your day. Whether you are having a bad day at work or a great day all together, notice how you deal with things like social pressure, testing situations and people overall. Our mental framework shapes the frequency of our vibrational energy. Never underestimate the power of the mind or the power people have over your thoughts and mind, if you allow them. Always be aware.

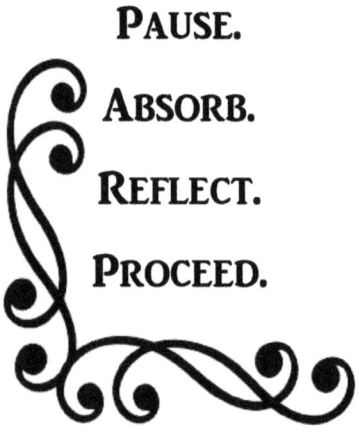

Pause.
Absorb.
Reflect.
Proceed.

Our daily activities have been amplified due to evolution. With that said, self-reflection is pivotal! We have become busier than ever before. Thus, reflecting on the aspects of our lives that help us align our energy to find our balance is critical. What reflecting also does, is give us an opportunity to evaluate which behaviours we do need to keep and which we need to work on eliminating. Therefore, you need to hold yourself accountable for every action you take and to be able to acknowledge things you need to change and implement accordingly.

Self-belief is the first step to condition others to believe in you. I have heard the saying "you cannot expect someone to love you if you do not love yourself first". This may be considered has the hardest thing to do, but I assure you it is possible. Once you attain this self-belief power within you, it will be easy to carry it over to another. This must be a daily routine, as there is sometimes just too little love that is shared out there.

PUT YOUR DREAMS INTO ACTION. SIMPLY DREAMING IS NOT ENOUGH

This is not about just dreaming; it is about transforming your dreams into reality. If you do not take action towards achieving your dreams, you will regret it in time. Because it is not enough to just have a dream, you have to believe in that dream and believe in yourself too. When you know you can do it, you will do it. And that's the difference between you and dreamers. You are going to achieve great things because you are great and you believe it. The road to success may not be easy, but once you have reached the top, you will realize it was all worth it. Never stop dreaming if you plan on achieving those dreams.

ACKNOWLEDGE SMALL VICTORIES

Imagine you are playing at the beach and your aim is to build a sand castle. That is your end goal. First you need to find the correct sand. Then you need to find a place on the beach. And as small or insignificant as these few steps may seem, if not done correctly it could cost you your entire sand castle. Be proud and acknowledge your small achievements all the way. Apply this to your daily life and view it as steps towards self-love. We underestimate the power of self-love. However, self-love and acknowledging your victories (no matter how small) are very powerful methods to raise our vibrations.

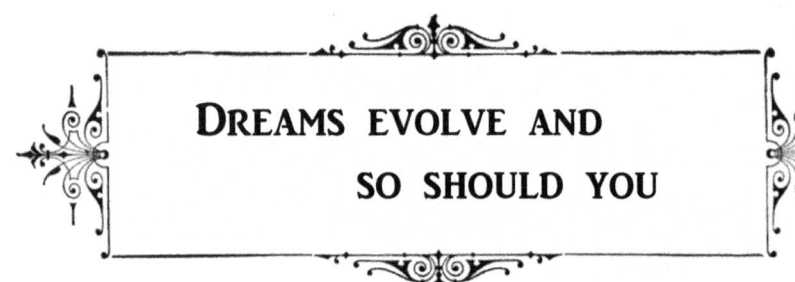

This particular one is as important as every other one, but perhaps in fewer words. Dreams, like goals, also change along the way. Adapting to these changes is progress and will allow you to evolve in the same way your dreams may evolve. You have to allow yourself to grow beyond the comfort zone you may have created by following a particular dream. Break away from that and challenge yourself to do more, and to be more.

Life is a series of do's and don'ts, there are certain things you do and certain things you don't. For example; do aim high no matter the risk and don't give up, no matter how hard. Because life will throw a curveball at you, and sometimes at every turn. You may dodge a few but if you get knocked down by one, remember to not let it keep you down. You have to get back up. Dust off your bruises (you may need them later), fix your outfit and carry on moving. Whatever you do, do not give up. Because you never know how close you really are. For example; the average safe diving depth is between 18-20 meters. More than 20 meters is known as deep sea diving. When a diver goes beyond 20 meters deep, they will start to experience a lot of internal pressure around the ears and chest. Making it nearly impossible to breath, let alone continue swimming. And most divers give the signal to go back up the deeper they dive. Without realizing that they are literally 1 meter away from the bottom of the ocean. Before you consider giving up, first take a moment to see how far you have come. Because sometimes, no matter how unbearable it becomes, you may only be one step away from achieving your goals and living out your dreams.

This is about being a master of more than one thing or skill. This could be in business or life in general. You should afford yourself with a bigger platform in life by doing as many things as possible, but with great responsibility and dedication. Establish what you are good at, divide your time accordingly and in such a way that it allows you full capacity to do your work well at all times. Do not fool yourself for that may be very limiting to you. When it comes to business, spread yourself across different target markets. Spread out your income achievement flow and in terms of your life, balance out your energy to gratify more than just your mind.

Live your dreams, because no-one is going to do it for you

This is about taking ownership of your dreams. What is your dream? And how do you plan on living it out? This is a question many of us get to at some point in our lives, and some of us are clear about what our dreams are. But what use is a clear dream if you don't take ownership of it. Living your own dream is crucial to being true to yourself. It may have the support of many around you, but without truly investing your mind and emotions into owning your dream, your dream will always be just that…A DREAM.

No matter where you are in your life, there are circles of influence around you. Sometimes you will not know who the circle of influence was until you dig deep in your memories to find them. The task here is to never forget those who were there when you started. Yes, some will have served their purpose and have slowly made their way out of your life, and then there are those who are still influencing, supporting and even believing in you today. Everyone in your life, no matter how briefly they have been there, has an influence on your life and even the lessons you learn. Those who are with you through thick and thin are the ones who should be acknowledged. This acknowledgment can be a simple 'Thank You' and by showing them gratitude.

NEVER UNDERESTIMATE
THE POWER OF
QUIET TIME
AND
SELF REFLECTION

What if I told you that quiet time is not just about refreshing, but it is also an opportunity to love yourself and even problem solve what you may be going through? When people hear "quiet time" there is a misconception that this had to take the form of meditation. Quiet time could be taking a drive, or a walk, spending time away from family or a spouse for the night or even just a few hours. Quiet time is really an opportunity to love yourself and also reflect on where you are in your life, what your next steps are and just acknowledging that loving yourself is a great starting point. If you are stuck in a dead-end job or are really unhappy doing what you do for a living, then you are actually letting yourself down and no-one else. Take time to get to know you again, so that you may refocus your energy on something more positive and promising.

> **LOVE WHAT YOU DO BECAUSE YOU OWE IT TO YOURSELF**

Love what you do by doing what you love. You were created with talents like no other, and the skill to enhance those talents through learning and observation. You owe it to yourself to be happy, so why not start with your career. If you are stuck in a job that is hiding your talents, then you need to leave. It may take you 5 months or 5 years to leave, but if you want it bad enough, it will happen no matter how long you have to wait. Keep encouraging yourself to accept a future filled with possibilities and a future that doesn't require you to do something you hate. And it will come true.

YOU ARE YOUR BUSINESS

The truth is, no-one else knows you better than you know yourself. And you are whoever you say you are. So, if you want to feel good, treat yourself good. If you want to be great, then treat yourself great. And if you want to be successful, then you have to treat yourself to success. It's no-one's business what you do, when you do or how you do it. It's your business. So, treat yourself like you are the business you want to own one day. With respect, loyalty, good work ethics, conduct and code, and everyone who sees you will follow suit. You are no body's business but your own.

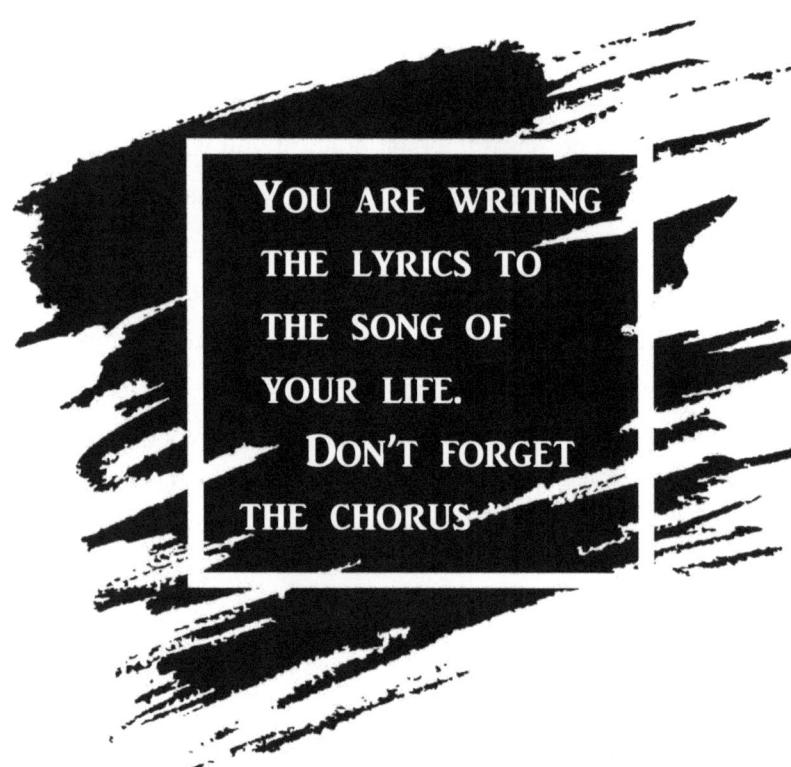

When listening to a song the part that sticks with you the most is the chorus. This can be applied to your life if you view your life as a song. What you want to resonate and be remembered for is the chorus, so make sure it is a good one. The beat of your life depends a lot on the choices you make or don't make. If you had to view your life's lyrics, make sure the lyrics are something that you can be proud of so that when people 'sing' these lyrics they truly define who you are. Don't forget, everything that you do creates an impact, much like in the way a chorus does in a song. So, don't just do your life, rather live your life so that your chorus can be repeated for years to come. Something you can be proud of.

Some may slow you down. You can choose to allow it, or not

We meet many people during the course of our lives; some people are on the same level as we are while others are on a different level. This is about being aware of who is on the same level as you and who may be holding you back from achieving greatness. This is not about cutting those people out of your life, but rather about being aware of where you stand with others. This is also about putting yourself in the position where you can be surrounded by people with a higher energy level so that you can learn from them and grow. One thing that is for certain, it's that the experience you gain cannot be taken away. Specific educated people may not have the experience that you have. This can be seen as an advantage both in business and life in general. For example; take someone who has a Doctorate in Business and someone who has no degree. The person in business may be great at what they do but have no people skills, and the person without a degree may be great in their company's business because they have people skills. It doesn't matter what your background is or what you have achieved, what matters is what you do with what you have. And I say, make the most of the little you have.

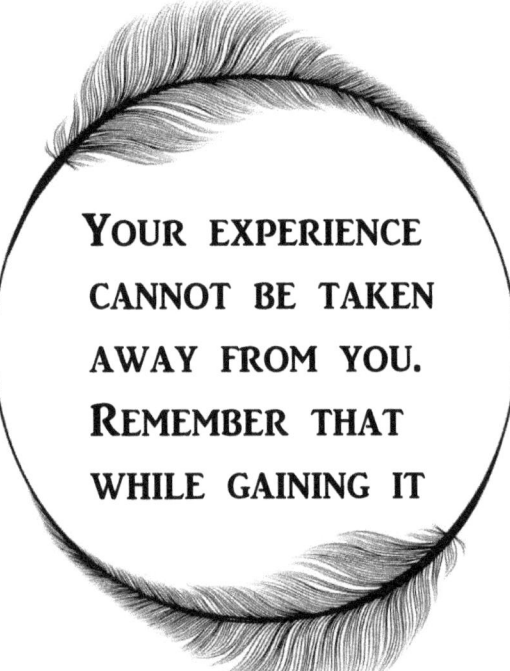

Your experience cannot be taken away from you. Remember that while gaining it

Never forget that learning something new can never be taken away from you, no matter who you are or how old you are. Avoid being stuck in your comfort zone as this can be dangerous, because you then follow a daily routine instead of living your life to the fullest and allowing yourself to experience new things and new approaches. Something my parents taught me is to grab as many opportunities as possible. With different opportunities, come different challenges and overcoming these challenges comes growth, and with growth comes wisdom. Therefore, never deprive your mind of new experiences by not coming out of your comfort zone. Do the same for your energy. Both of these thrive on evolution and transcendence. Be ready, be open and embrace each and every opportunity that comes your way.

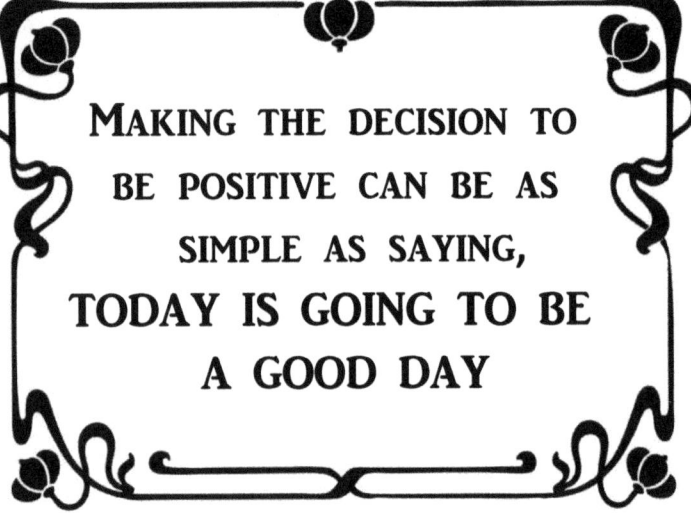

Making the decision to be positive can be as simple as saying, today is going to be a good day

This particular one is about how to react when we find it hard to produce positive vibrations during our day. We ought to find it within ourselves, to say words like "Today is going to be a good day!" Repeat this a few times and anchor the belief that your day will be good. You must convince your whole being by conditioning yourself. As much as we may not want to believe it, we often need convincing because we are vulnerable to negative vibrations as mentioned above. Saying that the day is going to be good, is a good way to start the day. There is nothing stopping you from repeating this to yourself during the day. And yes, we must continuously convince ourselves. A lot of this is pure self-belief, and it is important for your positive energy levels.

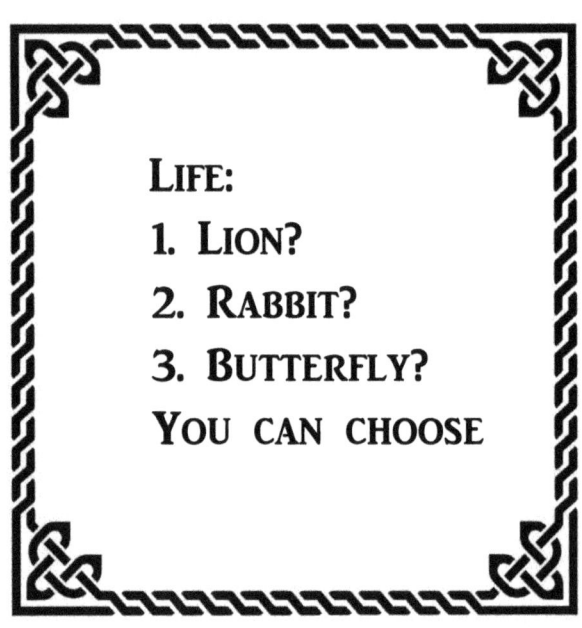

LIFE:
1. LION?
2. RABBIT?
3. BUTTERFLY?
YOU CAN CHOOSE

The choices we make in life define who we are as individuals. So, the question is, who do you see yourself as? A Lion? The King of the Beasts. A boss in his/her own right and a leader to many? Or do you see yourself as a little Rabbit? Prey to all other predators. Scared and timid but quick to respond to danger. Always battling to survive no matter the circumstance. Or do you consider yourself to be a beautiful Butterfly? Who started off as a Caterpillar, then transitioned into a Cocoon of wonder before breaking free as the Butterfly that you always envisioned? And even though most days you feel small and insignificant, you are powerful enough to create and leave an impact. Whatever you choose, make sure it is the right choice for you. No matter what it is, if it is the right choice for you, you will excel at everything you do.

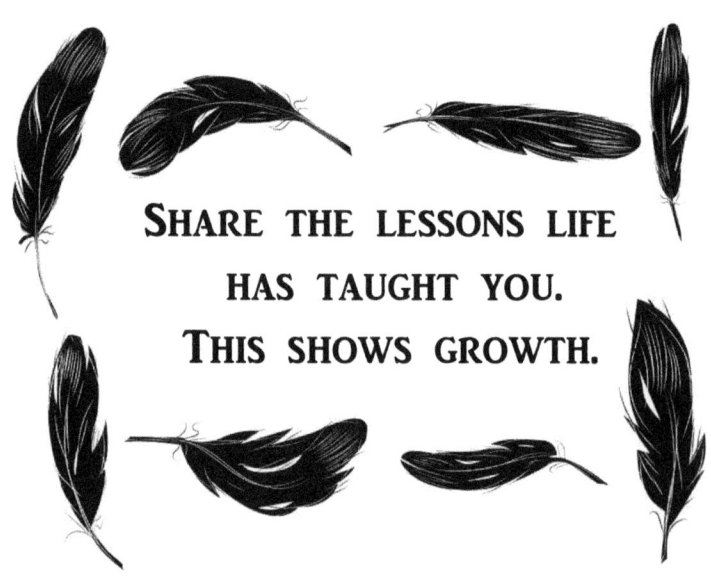

Share the lessons life has taught you. This shows growth.

I encourage you to share what you learn throughout life. This is not to show off in any way, but rather to share with those that cannot obtain the same experience or knowledge for whatever reason. You will be surprised how much appreciation you can get by sharing your experiences and knowledge. Always remember that everyone is going through their own journey. And sometimes hearing someone else's experience through their journey, can boost you through yours. All you can do is guide and share, even though you may be criticized by some, don't be discouraged.

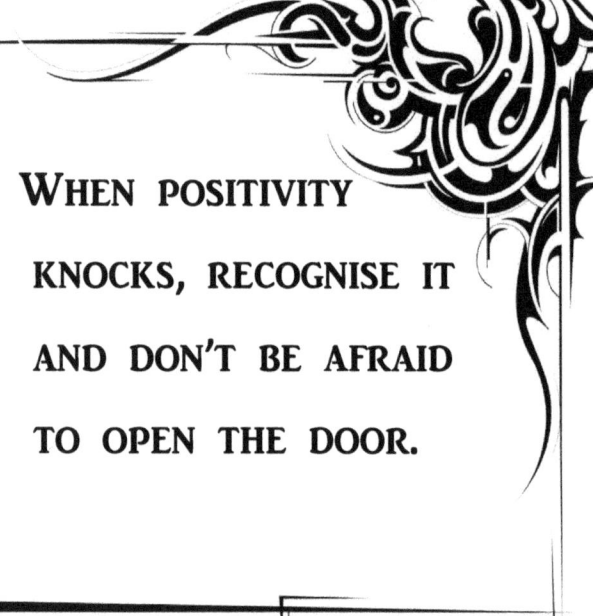

When positivity knocks, recognise it and don't be afraid to open the door.

Ever heard someone say, "Things are going so well, something must go wrong…" This is an example of how negativity can creep within your great efforts. So do not let the negativity creep in. In fact, never allow negative vibes cause a shift in your positive mindset. Letting your energy succumb to negativity is a waste of time and it can be damaging to your mindset. That is why I say, when something positive comes along, you first have to recognize it as something positive and not something negative covered by positivity. For example; don't sacrifice your loyalty for the job of your dreams. Find another way that won't question your integrity. Another example would be, doing something that you don't really have to do but want to do to prove someone else wrong. It is a waste of time and can drain what's left of your positive energy. Even though it may be a good thing for you, it comes from a negative place, so nothing good will come of it.

TREAT EVERY DAY WITH THE ENERGY OF A FRIDAY

Every day is a special day. It all just depends on what energy you embody. There is something truly amazing about the energy people have on a Friday. It is like the energy people have when it is payday or when they have won a prize or are surrounded by happy people. The power of channelling that amazing energy should never be underestimated. I encourage you to approach each day with the energy that you have on a Friday. Allow the energy to flow freely and do *not* allow negativity to creep in. Every day is Friday!! And as soon as you adopt this, your day, week, month and year will be exceptional.

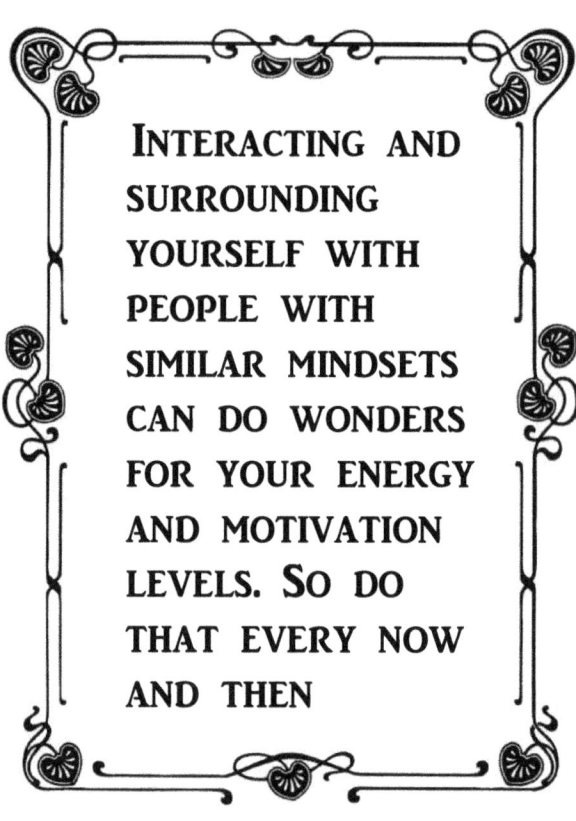

Interacting and surrounding yourself with people with similar mindsets can do wonders for your energy and motivation levels. So do that every now and then

Always be aware of your surroundings, some situations were designed to build you up and others may be there with the sole purpose of breaking you down. Know the difference. When you feel unfavourable energies surround you from a particular situation, I suggest you trust your instincts, and leave as soon as you can. But when you feel favourable energies of encouragement surround you from a particular situation, I suggest you use that to your advantage to learn and grow to the best of your ability.

There are many ideas out there and some of these ideas are great! And many times, these great ideas are forgotten along the way. There is no point in having great ideas without making the efforts to put these ideas into action. You must implement these ideas, nurture them and constantly monitor their growth or outcome. Therefore, just like seeds, you need fertile ground. A strategic plan of action for implementation, the correct climate, water and great care as the plan of action before planting them. An excellent harvest will depend entirely on how you will care and grow your idea, so it will be of high importance to monitor, follow through and take ownership to ensure a successful outcome. Therefore, when you decide to create an idea and bring it into existence, do it wholeheartedly. The greater danger is ending up living a life that floats from day to day without purpose or acknowledging any of your gifts and talents throughout life.

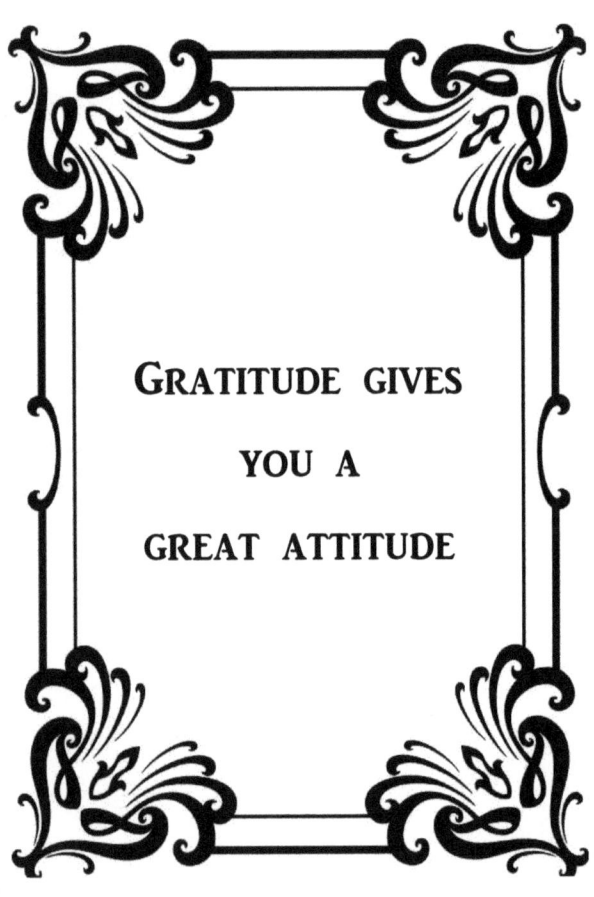

GRATITUDE GIVES YOU A GREAT ATTITUDE

This is about acknowledging the gifts we receive and appreciating the little and big things in life. When we are appreciative of the gifts from life we start to live better. Simply lay in bed at night, before you go sleep, count your blessings. This does not have to be material things, because truth is, material things are not an example of blessings. Your good health is an example. Your husband or wife lying next to you is an example. Your child or children in the next room is an example. The business deal you just closed, the exam you just passed, the promotion you just received at work, and the approval for your home loan are examples of good blessings. Do not confuse blessings with material things, because material things are only the by-product of those blessings. Be thankful for the door that opened and the opportunity that presented itself through that opened door. Once you recognise the root of your blessings, your gratitude will transform to new heights, leaving you with a better life lived.

This is about losing the sense of regret for missed opportunities. The last thing you want is to find yourself sitting on a rocking chair, retired, asking yourself, "What would have happened if I took that job..." or "What would have happened if I decided to give up everything to travel..." and so on. When a great opportunity presents itself, seize the moment. Life is shorter than we want to believe it to be. Therefore, be certain to live your best life as much as you can. Be good to yourself because your life is yours to live. You have every chance to become great, so strive for spiritual contentment and be satisfied with the life you have while achieving your goals.

SATISFACTION CREATES COMFORT ZONES DON'T GET STUCK

What we do not realize is that when you choose to glide through life without taking risks, you are actually in a comfort zone. You must break beyond your comfort and give yourself the opportunity to experience new things. This may seem scary at first, but anxiety should never hold you back from accepting the challenge of pursuing things that are intriguing. Better to Learn, Grow and Explore.

* * *

A Letter to You

I hope that this book has brought you inspiration and motivation for daily, weekly or even constant use. Be sure to share your life lessons and #SUNNYMOTIV quotes with your family and friends, so that they too can benefit from it. This book has been designed in such a way that you can read through it any which way you want. Let your inner light guide you. I am pleased that you have immersed yourself in this book and I wish each and every one of you love, joy and peace for many years to come.

Keep smiling, be happy, awaken your soul, and exercise self-love.

Contact details

Contact me directly for any clarity or guidance about any one of the #SUNNYMOTIVs;

Sunil Osman
Website: www.sunilosman.com
https://linktr.ee/sunilosman
E-mail: sunnymotiv@sunilosman.com

www.ingramcontent.com/pod-product-compliance
Lightning Source LLC
Chambersburg PA
CBHW050815090426
42736CB00021B/3457